MOOSE

Jen Green

Grolier
an imprint of
SCHOLASTIC
www.scholastic.com/librarypublishing

Published 2008 by Grolier
An imprint of Scholastic Library Publishing
Old Sherman Turnpike, Danbury,
Connecticut 06816

For The Brown Reference Group plc
Project Editor: Jolyon Goddard
Copy-editors: Ann Baggaley, Lisa Hughes
Picture Researcher: Clare Newman
Designers: Jeni Child, Lynne Ross,
    Sarah Williams
Managing Editor: Bridget Giles

Volume ISBN-13: 978-0-7172-6270-0
Volume ISBN-10: 0-7172-6270-7

**Library of Congress
Cataloging-in-Publication Data**

Nature's children. Set 3.
    p. cm.
  Includes bibliographical references and
  index.
  ISBN 13: 978-0-7172-8082-7
  ISBN 10: 0-7172-8082-9
  1. Animals--Encyclopedias, Juvenile. 1.
  Grolier Educational (Firm)
  QL49.N384 2008
  590.3--dc22
                    2007031568

Printed and bound in China

PICTURE CREDITS

Front Cover: **Corbis**: George D. Lepp.

Back Cover: **Nature PL**: Staffan Widstrand;
Shutterstock: Jessica Bilen, Ronnie
Howard, Reston Images.

Corbis: John Conrad 9, Momatiuk-Eastcott
37; **FLPA**: Mark Newman 41, Michael
Quinton 29; **Nature PL**: Pete Cairns 46,
Asgeir Helgestad 10, Steven Kazlowski 2–3,
5, 38, Tom Mangelsen 6, Jeff Vanuga 26–27;
Photolibrary.com: Stan Osolinski 33,
James T. Stachecki 45; **Shutterstock**: 4,
Wesley Aston 17, Jason Cheeves 34,
FloridaStock 30, Roman Krochuk 18,
Wendy Nero 22; **Still Pictures**: Patrick
Frischknecht 13, 14, S. Meyers 21;
Superstock: Mark Newman 42.

Contents

Fact File: Moose 4

Shaky Start 7

Biggest Deer 8

Moose Country 11

Hot to Trot? 12

Heavy Headgear 15

Changing Antlers 16

Handlebars 19

Standing Tall 20

The Moose Is Loose 23

Woolly Coat 24

Serious Eaters 25

Feature Photo 26–27

Winter Feeding 28

Chewing the Cud 31

Tuning In 32

Water Lovers 35

Getting Along 36

Finding a Partner 39

Newborn Moose 40

Walking on Stilts 43

Swimming Lessons 44

Strangers Beware! 47

Life Lessons 48

   Words to Know 49

   Find Out More 51

   Index 52

FACT FILE: Moose

Class	Mammals (Mammalia)
Order	Cloven-hoofed mammals (Artiodactyla)
Family	Deer family (Cervidae)
Genus	*Alces*
Species	Moose (*Alces alces*)
World distribution	Found in northern North America, Europe, and Asia
Habitat	Northern forests, usually near water; also in woodlands and on the tundra in summer
Distinctive physical characteristics	A large deer with long ears, strong shoulders, and long legs. The male has large branching antlers and a fold of skin below his throat
Habits	Active by day; moose are solitary in summer but gather in small groups in winter; they wade or swim in lakes to feed and to escape from insects; the female raises her calves alone
Diet	Leaves, twigs, bark, grass, moss, lichen, shrubs, and water plants

Introduction

Nearly everything about a moose is surprising. With its huge body supported by long, stiltlike legs—and the enormous **antlers** on the male—it might look awkward when standing still. But a moose on the move is smooth and graceful. Moose are wonderful swimmers, too, and they can dive right under the water. During the icy northern winters these giant deer survive on the nourishment of twigs alone. Unlike most deer they do not live in herds.
A moose prefers to be alone.

Only male moose have antlers.

Moose calves
usually have rusty
red coats, which
later turn duller
and darker.

Shaky Start

A baby moose is called a **calf**. For the first week of its life, the calf's biggest problem is learning to walk. Baby moose have long, lanky, wobbly legs. As the new calf staggers about, its shaky legs threaten at every step to fold up and collapse beneath the young moose.

However, like all babies in the wild, the little moose must develop quickly in order to flee from dangerous enemies. By the second week the calf is not only used to walking, but has also learned to run. A two-week-old baby moose will have most likely already been swimming, too. In fact, all moose are very good swimmers.

Biggest Deer

Moose belong to the deer family. There are
about 45 different species, or types, of deer.
They are found nearly all over the world. North
American deer include moose, Virginia—or
white-tailed—deer, mule deer, and caribou.
Deer come in all shapes and sizes. The smallest
types, like the muntjac, are only about the size
of a German shepherd dog. The moose is the
biggest deer in the world—as big as a horse. It's
also one of the largest animals in North America.

The early ancestors of the moose lived in the
part of the world now called Asia. Around two
million years ago, these early moose made their
way to North America. They crossed the ice that
once covered much of the sea.

Male moose, like
nearly all their
deer relatives,
have antlers.

Moose vary in
size and color
depending on
where they live.
This one lives
in Norway.

Moose Country

Moose live across much of northern North America, including Alaska and most of Canada. In many areas they are common. They are also found in northern Europe, but there they are called elk. From Europe, moose country continues eastward right across northern Asia.

Moose are mostly forest-dwelling animals. They live in the vast band of conifer forest that stretches like a wide green belt across North America, Europe, and Siberia. Moose also live in woodlands where there are other types of trees, such as aspen and birch. They like to live close to water, including rivers, streams, lakes, and marshes. But some moose roam the windswept, treeless plains of the **tundra**, along with their deer relatives, the caribou.

Hot to Trot?

One of the most astonishing things about a moose is its size. These animals are as big as horses. A grown-up male, called a **bull**, stands more than 6 feet (1.85 m) tall at the shoulder, and weighs 1,200 to 1,600 pounds (540–720 kg). The female, or **cow**, may be only half as big. She usually weighs about 880 pounds (400 kg).

The moose is not the most attractive animal in the forest. It has mulelike ears, a long nose that ends in a square muzzle, huge nostrils, and rubbery lips. The bull has a flap of skin that hangs from his throat, called a **bell**. His powerful shoulders make him look a little hump-backed. The moose's long, barrel-like body ends in neat hindquarters and a short tail. Despite its awkward, clumsy appearance, a moose can move silently, easily, and often very quickly around its forest home.

An adult bull moose stands in the grasses of the tundra.

The exact shape of
the antlers and the
way the spiky points
grow are different
on each moose.

Heavy Headgear

For a few months every year, a bull moose carries a heavy weight on his head. His wide, branching antlers—which are made of bone—can weigh more than 60 pounds (30 kg) and measure up to 6.5 feet (2 m) across. Up to 30 points, called **tines**, stick up from the flattened, wing-shaped bases. A big bull's antlers are often as broad as the moose is tall.

Carrying such an enormous load does not trouble the powerful bull moose in the slightest. He can run fast and he can move through the thickest forest without catching his antlers on trees and bushes.

Changing Antlers

In winter, it is more difficult to tell bulls and cows apart. That is because the male has lost his antlers. Like other deer, moose shed their antlers as winter approaches. Often one antler drops off before the other. The bull then looks, and might feel, lopsided until the other antler drops off, too.

In spring, the male's antlers start to sprout again. They first appear as small black knobs on his forehead. The growing antlers are covered with a furry skin called **velvet**. The velvet carries blood to the antlers and helps them to grow.

In summer, when the antlers have grown to their full size, the velvet falls off. The bull looks very ragged while the pieces of dead skin hang from the new antlers. If the velvet does not fall off on its own, the moose will rub his antlers against trees until all the skin is removed. In the fall, when it's the **mating season**, the bull uses his antlers to impress the females and to frighten other males away. Once the mating season is over, the antlers are no longer needed.

16

This bull moose is shedding the velvet from his antlers.

Growing antlers requires a lot of nutrients. A bull moose needs a diet with plenty of calcium.

Handlebars

It takes about seven years for a moose's antlers to reach full size. A young moose's antlers start off very small. Each year they grow a little bigger than the previous year's antlers.

During his first year, the bull calf's antlers are just tiny stubs. The following year they stick out from his head like bicycle handlebars. Each year the antlers develop more and more, matching the growth of the rest of the young moose's body. Only when a male moose is full grown will he carry a set of broad, sweeping antlers. By then he is ready to find a mate and needs to be able to hold his own against other bulls. He can at last put his antlers to good use.

Standing Tall

The moose has long, gangly legs, which account for much of its height. The animal has a long stride, too. That helps it to step over obstacles such as fallen trees in the forest, without wasting a lot of energy by jumping.

Like all members of the deer family, the moose's **hooves** are split into two toes. As the moose walks, the toes spread out to support the animal's great weight. That allows the moose to wade through deep snow or walk over muddy ground without sinking too deeply.

Being tall gives moose an advantage. They can easily reach leaves far above the heads of most other plant-eating animals.

A moose stands tall among the trees of its forest home.

A moose runs away
from an enemy.

The Moose Is Loose

A moose moves gracefully, despite its huge size. Its usual pace is a loose-limbed trot, but if it is alarmed, it can gallop away at up to 35 miles (55 km) per hour. Running at top speed, a moose can usually escape most **predators**.

If a moose is cornered by an enemy, those long legs and sharp hooves make very useful weapons. The moose can lash out with either front or back hooves to defend itself against enemies such as wolves. It rarely misses its target. Many predators have been badly injured by a well-aimed kick from a moose.

Neither running away nor fighting can help a moose much when being hunted by humans. In such cases, the animal must use its ability to disappear among the trees with stealth and silence. In both North America and Europe, moose are hunted in the fall for their antlers, which are prized as trophies. Moose are also sometimes hunted for meat. There are strict laws to control the number of moose that hunters are allowed to shoot.

Woolly Coat

A moose's thick coat keeps it warm during the icy northern winters. The coat is made of two layers. On the outside, there is an overcoat of long, coarse hairs, called **guard hairs**. Those protect the moose from snow, wind, and rain. Beneath the guard hairs is an undercoat of dense, woolly fur. The undercoat acts like a warm vest, trapping air next to the moose's skin, which keeps in its body heat.

In summer, the moose's coat is thinner than it is in winter. Even so, the moose sometimes finds it difficult to stay cool. If the animal feels uncomfortable in the heat, it will stand for a while in deep water to cool down.

Serious Eaters

Moose spend much of their time eating. It takes a lot of plants to fuel that giant body. Moose usually eat in the early morning and again around dusk.

In summer, moose dine mainly on leaves, buds, and twigs. The food they love better than anything else is water lilies. In the early morning or late afternoon, they often wade chest-deep in water, **browsing** on water plants. They plunge their nose below the water and tear off the plants with their flexible lips.

Moose have teeth similar to other deer. They have no upper front teeth, just a hard, horny pad. The horny pad works well for crushing plant food to a pulp.

Two bull moose go
head to head in a fight.

Winter Feeding

The name *moose* is an Algonkian Native American word meaning "twig-eater." In winter, moose do indeed feed mostly on the twigs of trees such as willow, birch, and poplar. When the weather is cold and snow covers the ground, most other food is scarce. A full-grown moose can munch its way through 50 pounds (23 kg) of twigs in a single day.

In winter, just by looking at the trees, it is possible to tell if a moose has passed along that way. The lower branches of trees and bushes will have lost most of their twigs, up to a height of about 7 feet (2 m). That's as high as most moose can reach. If twigs are out of reach, a hungry moose will strip the bark from trees. These deer also feed on moss and **lichen** in winter.

A female moose munches on a winter meal of willow twigs.

Plant-eating animals such as the moose like to lie down while they chew the cud.

Chewing the Cud

Like all its deer relatives, the moose has a special stomach to help it digest tough, stringy plants. Moose have an extra chamber in their stomach that they use to store partly eaten food.

Moose and other deer chew their food not once, but twice. When the moose swallows a mouthful of leaves, the food is stored in the first part of its stomach. Later, when the moose is resting quietly, it brings the food back up into its mouth in order to chew it some more. This is called chewing the **cud**. When the twice-chewed food is gulped down again, it passes right through the stomach in the usual way. Chewing the cud helps the moose get the most nutrients out of its food.

Tuning In

The moose's big brown eyes are set at the sides of the animal's head. Moose can therefore see danger coming from almost any direction. Unfortunately, despite its large eyes a moose does not have very good eyesight. It relies on its other senses to find out all it needs to know.

The moose has an excellent sense of smell. Its keen nose quickly picks up the scent of predators, or anything unfamiliar that might be coming too close. A moose also has sharp hearing. Its long, mulelike ears can stand up or turn around to catch faint sounds on the breeze that might spell danger.

A moose may look calm, but it never stops twitching its ears for sounds or sniffing the air for scents of danger.

Taking high steps with their long legs, moose can walk nearly as easily in water as they can on land.

Water Lovers

Moose love to be near water. They love being in it even more. In summer, water means a good supply of food. Moose are strong swimmers and are known to dive right underwater to tear off water plants. When the moose goes under, its nostrils close tightly, like a submarine's hatches, to keep the water out.

Moose also use rivers or lakes to escape from the clouds of black flies and mosquitoes that pester them in summer. A moose will wade in the water up to its neck in order to hide from the buzzing insects. Wallowing in the mud also helps make its coat more insect-proof.

Getting Along

For most of the year, except for a short time during the mating season, moose are loners. They go about their lives without the company of their own kind.

However, in winter, moose sometimes gather in groups as they look for food. As they paw at the snow to uncover plants, the ground gets stomped down. These flattened areas are called "**yards**." Even in yards, moose tend to keep their distance. They don't help one another or get too friendly. In fact, the biggest and strongest animals tend to be bullies. They muscle in on the best spots and take the largest share of the food.

When they meet, young bull moose might take the opportunity to practice their sparring.

Well matched in size, two big bulls square up to battle over a female.

Finding a Partner

Fall is the mating season for moose. This season is also called the **rut**. For the solitary moose, finding a partner, especially in dense forest, might seem difficult. But moose have ways of attracting their mates. As the female wanders through the forest, she makes loud calls. Her scent, which changes during the mating season, also lets the males know she is ready to find a partner.

When two males answer the cow's call at the same time, there can be trouble. Each bull tries to scare away the other by showing off his big antlers. If neither bull backs down, the two may have a pushing contest. Moose don't charge at each other. If they did, their antlers might lock together—and if they couldn't break free they might starve to death. While these "bull fights" might look scary, they usually end without either moose getting seriously hurt.

Newborn Moose

About eight months after mating, the female moose prepares to give birth. Cows are very picky about where they give birth. They look for a safe spot in dense forest, often near water. An island is one of the best places for a nursery.

The cow might have a single calf, but two or three young are also common. A newborn moose weighs 22 to 35 pounds (10–16 kg). The calf lies on the ground while the mother licks it. Soon the baby finds its mother's milk and begins to drink.

Bull moose take no part in raising their offspring. The cow gives birth and raises her youngsters without help.

A mother moose gently encourages her new baby to get to its feet.

41

A moose calf grows fast.
It might gain as much as
one pound (0.5 kg) a day.

Walking on Stilts

A moose calf is born with its eyes open and woolly fur covering its body. It spends its first day or two lying on the ground, being nuzzled by its mother. But around day three, the mother nudges it with her long nose, to encourage it to stand.

Seeing a baby moose take its first tottering steps is like watching someone trying to walk on stilts. But the calf doesn't take long to learn how to use its long, wobbly legs.

Within a few days, the calf is ready for its first outing with its mother. It goes with her as she wanders from the nursery. Before long, the baby starts to nibble plants, following the cow's example. However, it continues to drink its mother's milk until it is about six months old.

Swimming Lessons

Adult moose are expert swimmers. A full-grown moose can swim at up to 6 miles (9.5 km) an hour—that's about as fast as a human can jog. During a calf's first week, its mother leads it down to a lake or river and lets it get used to the water. The calf soon becomes skilled at paddling about, while holding its head high out of the water.

If you see two moose swimming, one will probably be a calf, and the other its mother. If the calf gets tired, it takes a break, resting its nose on its mother's back. After a "breather," it gets its strength back and starts paddling again.

Young moose calves become at home in the water when they are just a few days old.

Running with its mother, this young moose is now fast and strong enough to escape predators.

Strangers Beware!

A full-grown moose has little to fear from predators. However, a newborn calf is at risk of being attacked by a bear or a wolf, and some youngsters do get killed. But a hungry predator has to get past the mother moose first.

If a predator appears, the cow rushes in front of her calf, lowering her head and stamping her feet. She snorts in rage and rears up on her hind legs, pawing the air with her hooves. Faced with this scary sight, many predators run quickly in the opposite direction.

If the calf's own father approaches, he gets exactly the same treatment as a predator. It is also very dangerous for humans to get close to a female and her calf. The safest rule is for all strangers to keep their distance from moose mothers and their young.

Life Lessons

The calf stays close to its mother throughout summer and fall. By copying its mother, the calf learns which trees have tasty bark, and how to pull up water lilies. It sees how the cow reacts to danger. When winter comes it learns to cope with the cold. All these lessons are important if the youngster is to live a long life. Moose can survive for more than 20 years in the wild.

When warm weather returns in spring, the mother prepares to give birth again. It is then time for the young moose to go off on its own. It won't be very long before a young female moose herself becomes a mother, usually at the age of three years old. Young bulls don't become fathers until the age of five or six, by which time their antlers are well grown.

Words to Know

Antlers	The bony branches on a male moose's head.
Bell	The flap of skin under a male moose's throat.
Browsing	Feeding on plants.
Bull	A male moose.
Calf	A young moose.
Cow	A female moose.
Cud	Half-chewed plant food that returns to the mouth for chewing again.
Guard hairs	The long, coarse hairs that form an animal's outer coat.
Lichen	A moss-like growth on rocks and trees.

Hooves	The feet of an animal such as a deer or a cow.
Mating season	The time of year when animals come together to produce young.
Predators	Animals that hunt other animals for food.
Rut	The breeding season for moose.
Tines	The curving points on a moose's antlers.
Tundra	The flat, treeless plains of the north.
Velvet	The soft, furry skin that covers a moose's antlers as they grow.
Yards	Areas where moose gather to feed in winter.

Find Out More

Books

Dutemple, L. A. *North American Moose*. Nature Watch. Minneapolis, Minnesota: Lerner Publications, 2000.

Squire, A. *Moose*. True Books. Danbury, Connecticut: Children's Press, 2007.

Web sites

Enchanted Learning: Moose
www.enchantedlearning.com/subjects/mammals/deer/Mooseprintout.shtml
Facts about the moose and a diagram to print.

Moose
http://animals.nationalgeographic.com/animals/mammals/moose.html
Information about the moose.

Index

A, B

antlers 5, 9, 14, 15, 16, 17, 18, 19, 23, 39, 48

bell 12

birth 40, 48

browsing 25

bull 12, 13, 15, 16, 17, 18, 19, 26, 37, 38, 39, 40, 48

C, D

calf 19, 40, 41, 42, 43, 44, 45, 46, 47, 48

coat 6, 24

cow 12, 29, 39, 40, 41, 43, 46, 47, 48

cud 30, 31

deer 5, 8, 11, 20, 25, 31

diving 5, 35

E, F

ears 12, 32, 33

elk 11

enemies 7, 23

eyes 32, 43

eyesight 32

fall 16, 39, 48

feeding 20, 25, 28, 35, 36, 43

fighting 26, 38, 39

forest 11, 12, 15, 20, 21, 39

G, H

guard hairs 24

habitat 11

hearing 32

height 12, 20

hooves 20, 23, 47

L, M, N

legs 5, 7, 20, 23, 34, 43, 47

lichen 28

life span 48

mating season 16, 36, 39

milk 40, 43

moss 28

muzzle 12

nose 12, 25, 43, 44

nursery 40, 43

P

plants 25, 31, 36, 43

predators 23, 32, 46, 47

R, S, T

running 7, 15, 22, 23

rut 39

smell 32, 33

species 8

speed 23

spring 16

summer 16, 24, 25, 35, 48

swimming 5, 7, 35, 44

teeth 25

tines 15

toes 20

tundra 11, 13

twigs 28, 29

V, W, Y

velvet 16, 17

walking 7, 20, 34, 43

wallowing 35

water 5, 11, 24, 25, 34, 35, 40, 43, 44, 45

water lilies 25, 48

weight 12, 15, 20, 40

winter 5, 16, 24, 28, 29, 36, 48

yards 36